DISABILITIES CAN'T STOP US!

SHAQUEM GRIFFIN
Don't Tell Me What I Can't Do

Shannon H. Harts

PowerKiDS press.

New York

Published in 2021 by The Rosen Publishing Group, Inc.
29 East 21st Street, New York, NY 10010

Copyright © 2021 by The Rosen Publishing Group, Inc.

First Edition

Editor: Elizabeth Krajnik
Book Design: Reann Nye

Photo Credits: Series art (background) Ratana21/Shutterstock.com; cover Otto Greule Jr/Getty Images Sport/Getty Images; p. 5 Quinn Harris/Getty Images Sport/Getty Images; p. 7 Elaine Thompson/AP Images; p. 9 Ric Tapia/Icon Sportswire/Getty Images; p. 11 Kevin Mazur/Getty Images Entertainment/Getty Images; p. 13 Aaron M. Sprecher/AP Images; p. 15 Orlando Sentinel/Tribune News Service/Getty Images; p. 17 Streeter Lecka/Getty Images Sport/Getty Images; p. 19 John Raoux/AP Images; p. 21 Kevin C. Cox/Getty Images Sport/Getty Images; p. 23 Ben Liebenberg/AP Images; p. 25 Darron Cummings/AP Images; p. 26 Rob Leiter/Getty Images Sport/Getty Images; p. 27 Fort Worth Star-Telegram/Tribune News Service/Getty Images; p. 29 Paul Abell/AP Images; p. 30 Joe Robbins/Getty Images Sport/Getty Images.

Cataloging-in-Publication Data

Names: Harts, Shannon.
Title: Shaquem Griffin: don't tell me what I can't do / Shannon Harts.
Description: New York : PowerKids Press, 2021. | Series: Disabilities Can't stop us! | Includes glossary and index.
Identifiers: ISBN 9781725311107 (pbk.) | ISBN 9781725311121 (library bound) | ISBN 9781725311114 (6 pack)
Subjects: LCSH: Griffin, Shaquem, 1995—Juvenile literature. | Linebackers (Football)–United States–Biography–Juvenile literature. | Seattle Seahawks (Football team)–Juvenile literature. | Football players–United States–Biography–Juvenile literature.
Classification: LCC GV939.G754 2021 | DDC 796.332092 B–dc23

Manufactured in the United States of America

CPSIA Compliance Information: Batch #CSPK20. For Further Information contact Rosen Publishing, New York, New York at 1-800-237-9932.

CONTENTS

The Making of a Mission

Shaquem Griffin, a linebacker for the Seattle Seahawks of the National Football League (NFL), had his left hand **amputated** when he was four years old due to a **congenital** disorder. Griffin has never let that keep him from playing football.

Early in his life, Griffin didn't understand why people didn't want him to play football. He didn't feel he had a disability or a reason to be treated differently. When he was eight years old, a coach tried to keep Griffin out of a game that could take his team to the playoffs. Eventually, Griffin was allowed to play and caught an interception that secured his team's victory! This game sparked Griffin's desire to play football in the NFL and to use this platform to encourage young athletes with disabilities.

UNSTOPPABLE!

The odds of being drafted by an NFL team are low. Only about 9 out of every 10,000 high school football players will eventually play for an NFL team.

Griffin wrote about the football game that changed his life in an open letter to NFL general managers before the Seattle Seahawks drafted him.

Learning the Lingo

The following terms have to do with American football:

draft: A process through which sports teams take turns choosing from a pool of players.

general manager: The highest-standing person who works for a sports team and answers to the team's owner.

interception: When a player catches a pass meant for their opponent, resulting in their team gaining possession of the ball.

National Football League (NFL): A professional American football league made up of 32 teams.

A Rare Condition

Griffin was born July 20, 1995—less than two minutes after his twin brother Shaquill—into a hardworking family in Saint Petersburg, Florida. His mother, Tangie, was working as a nurse and his father, Terry, was working as a truck operator.

Tangie first found out there was a problem with one of her babies before they were born. An **ultrasound** showed that a part of her **womb** was wrapped around Shaquem's left wrist, cutting off the blood supply to his hand. This problem is called amniotic band syndrome.

The doctors feared that if they tried to fix it, part of the womb could wrap around one of the babies' necks instead. Knowing their child would likely have a malformed or nonexistent hand, the Griffins decided early on that they wouldn't treat him differently than their other children.

The Griffins taught their sons the importance of working hard to achieve their goals from an early age.

What Is Amniotic Band Syndrome?

Amniotic band syndrome is a rare condition that happens when parts of the womb become wrapped around parts of the baby. It occurs at a rate of 1 in 1,200 to 1 in 15,000 live births. It can cause different birth defects, or problems, such as fused fingers and toes. Its effects can range from mild—involving fingers or toes—to severe—involving the head. Babies with amniotic band syndrome may require treatment in the form of surgery after they're born.

Pushing Through the Pain

When Shaquem was born, his left hand hadn't developed completely. Even the slightest bump to his hand would bring **intense** pain. One night when he was just four years old, Shaquem was in so much pain that he tried to cut his fingers off with a knife, but his mother stopped him. The next day, Tangie took him to the hospital to have his hand amputated.

Even though he only had one hand, Shaquem learned how to do everything other kids were doing. He could tie his shoes, climb trees, and play football. The day after his surgery, Shaquem played football and got blood all over his bandage. Shaquem's parents considered getting him a **prosthetic** hand, but they decided against it because he didn't seem to need it.

UNSTOPPABLE!

At first, the doctor told Tangie that Shaquem would need to wait a month before getting his hand amputated. However, she told them that Shaquem's pain was too intense and he couldn't wait that long. His surgery happened the next day.

Shaquem Griffin

Shaquill Griffin

Shaquem and Shaquill have always had a close bond. They learned to play catch with their dad. Shaquem said, "I took a couple footballs to the face before I learned to catch."

The Bond of Brothers

Growing up, Shaquem answered many questions from his classmates about what happened to his left hand. His parents raised him to be patient and kind. His mother has said that he'd often make jokes about his hand, such as saying a shark bit it off when it jumped into his boat while on a fishing trip.

Kids sometimes picked on Shaquem. A young girl once said his hand looked like a pickle. Shaquem took it as a joke, but Shaquill was mad. Shaquill always looked out for his brother. They were best friends throughout their childhood and grew to love football together. When the boys were eight years old, they vowed to stick together through everything and to chase their dream of playing together in the NFL.

UNSTOPPABLE!

In 2009, Shaquem and Shaquill formed a youth track club called Saint Pete Nitro in their hometown. The club was for more than just running. Kids got help with their homework and worked through problems at home.

Shaquem, left, and Shaquill, right, worked hard to create a club where kids felt safe. One of the managers of the team said, "Shaquem and Shaquill, their voice is so powerful within the community and the school."

Practicing with the Mad Scientist

Even though it wasn't easy, Shaquem was determined to learn to catch a football just as well as anyone with two hands. This required a lot of practice, but he never gave up. When practicing in their yard, Terry would throw the ball just as hard for Shaquem as for Shaquill. Shaquem worked on not relying solely on his right hand. He learned to punch the football with his left arm.

Terry had Shaquem go through all the same drills as Shaquill, but he would also find other ways of making sure Shaquem was just as challenged as his brother. Terry made contraptions, or unusual and useful devices, to help Shaquem almost "like a mad scientist," Tangie said in a 2017 interview.

UNSTOPPABLE!

Shaquem and Shaquill were high school football stars. Shaquem was known for his speed and strength. He earned the nickname "Beast" and was a team captain.

Part of what makes Griffin such a good player is that he knows everything there is to know about how football is played and that he has made the game work for him through many years of practice.

Training Inventions

Terry created ways for Shaquem to train with his brother even when certain exercises were difficult. He made something he called "the book," which was a piece of wood wrapped in cloth that Shaquem could attach to his lower left forearm. This invention was a sort of prosthetic hand that helped him do push-ups, curls, and bench presses. By the time he was in his last year of high school, Shaquem could bench press 260 pounds (117.9 kg).

Sticking Together

It didn't take long for colleges to start noticing Shaquill and Shaquem's skills on the football field. When they were in high school, the University of South Florida (USF) offered Shaquill his first **scholarship**, but they didn't offer one to Shaquem. Shaquill didn't take it. Instead, the twins went to the university's football camp in Tampa, Florida.

After arriving, Shaquill decided to sit out so Shaquem could be the focus. USF offered Shaquem a scholarship after watching him play during the camp, but he turned it down because he felt it was too late. The twins then visited the University of Central Florida (UCF) in Orlando. The head coach, George O'Leary, offered each of them a football scholarship. They accepted and enrolled in late summer 2013.

UNSTOPPABLE!

When the twins were 13, they promised each other they would go to the same college. Shaquill turned down a scholarship from the University of Miami—his dream school—so he and Shaquem could stick together.

Shaquem was a linebacker for the UCF Knights and Shaquill was a cornerback.

15

Upsetting Setbacks

While Shaquill found success on the football field during his college years, Shaquem was often on the bench. He kept getting **demoted** and wasn't told why. When he'd ask, coaches would often say things like, "your time will come" and "stay focused." Shaquem continued to work hard and he felt like he was improving, but he didn't get to travel much with the team for games.

After a few seasons, Shaquill was starting and Shaquem was backing up other players. Shaquem often felt discouraged, but he kept a lot of it to himself and remained supportive of his brother. He kept a positive attitude. Shaquem often lived through his brother, watching every game he could on TV or online.

Although Shaquem didn't see much time on the field when O'Leary was coaching the UCF Knights, things changed when the team hired a new head coach in late 2015.

>

Nothing Comes Easy

One of the toughest points in Shaquem's football career came the summer of 2015, before his third season at UCF. Shaquill stayed at school to continue training with the team at UCF and Shaquem was sent home.

That summer, Shaquem worked for his father's tow truck business and with his older brother Andre. From Monday through Saturday, he worked from 7 a.m. to 6 p.m., and then he'd go to his old high school to train with the track team. Later in the evening, he'd clean offices with Andre from 8 p.m. to midnight. Drained from working such long days, Shaquem thought about quitting football for good. Then he remembered the **pact** he'd made with his brother, who was on the way to achieving their goal, and he didn't give up.

One of the longest periods that Shaquem and Shaquill were apart was when Shaquem returned home to Saint Petersburg the summer before his third season at UCF.

>

Not So Fast

While working for his father's tow truck business, a man whose truck was being towed pulled out a $5 bill and offered it to Shaquem. Before Shaquem could take it, the man snatched it back and tore it in half. He gave Shaquem one half and said, "Keep on working, son, because nothing ever comes easy." Shaquem realized that to get what he wanted, he had to keep working as hard as he could.

Proving His Power

Scott Frost, the new head football coach at UCF, started in December 2015. He gave Shaquem a fresh start. Jovan DeWitt, another coach who came with Frost, said he didn't notice Shaquem had one hand until after drills ended and spring practice started. What he did notice, however, was Shaquem's speed. Shaquem was a quick and skilled player. He was moved to the starting lineup going into the 2016 season.

Shaquem also stood out for his toughness and how he avoided making excuses. He broke his right hand and still managed to play in a game in Houston, Texas. Because the coaches gave him more opportunities to play, Shaquem helped his team win a national championship title in 2017. In 2016, he was named the American Athletic Conference **defensive** player of the year.

UNSTOPPABLE!

Although he could get a disabled parking permit, Griffin declined one. He said of his hand, "It's not a deformity unless you make it one."

On January 1, 2018, Griffin helped the UCF Knights beat the Auburn University Tigers to win the Chick-fil-A Peach Bowl in Atlanta, Georgia.

Shaquem's College Awards

Shaquem earned a long list of awards while playing as a linebacker for the UCF Knights. Here are a few awards he received his senior year:

–2018 Uplifting Athletes Rare Disease Champion award

–ESPN All-Bowl Team honors

–Nominated for Allstate AFCA Good Works Team, honoring student-athletes for their outstanding community service

–Named to the 2017 American Athletic Conference All-Conference First Team

A Need for the NFL

Even though Shaquem won many awards and helped lead the UCF Knights to an undefeated season in 2017, he wasn't among the group of more than 300 college players invited to the 2018 NFL Scouting Combine. Shaquill was very upset. He was a star **rookie** with the Seattle Seahawks at the time. He felt Shaquem deserved an invite to the combine.

Shaquill publicly and privately **lobbied** for NFL coaches to give Shaquem a chance. After he was picked to play in the Senior Bowl, an event for the top senior college prospects, Shaquem received a late invitation to the combine on January 30, 2018. Shaquem knew he couldn't pass up the chance. It meant he could showcase his skills in front of some of the most influential people in football.

UNSTOPPABLE!

Limbitless Solutions is an organization that creates 3D-printed prosthetic limbs for children with limb differences. Griffin has spent time volunteering with Limbitless Solutions as well as working with them to better their prostheses.

One of the most important drills of the combine is the 40-yard dash. It can be the deciding factor for if a player is drafted.

What Is the NFL Scouting Combine?

The NFL Scouting Combine is a multiple-day event held annually at Lucas Oil Stadium in Indianapolis, Indiana. During this event, more than 300 college players go through many tests, including physical and mental exams, and are interviewed by people from a number of NFL teams. Then, players perform drills that have to do with the position they play. The combine is a chance for players to make an impression ahead of the NFL Draft.

Amazing Combine Performance!

Griffin made headlines and received national praise from the football community for the skills he showed at the combine. One of his most impressive feats was doing 20 repetitions, or repeats, of lifting 225 pounds (102.1 kg) on the bench press with a prosthetic hand. His initial goal was to do six repetitions. At training sessions in Texas before the combine, his personal record was 11 repetitions. However, with a crowd cheering him on, Shaquem beat his goal and was tied for 11th among the 25 linebackers who participated in the combine.

Griffin's 40-yard dash performance wowed many people watching—including Seattle Seahawks head coach Pete Carroll. Carroll later said that Griffin also did a great job at his interview with the NFL teams.

UNSTOPPABLE!

Before the combine, an NFL GM said he would be impressed if Shaquem could do five repetitions on the bench press with his prosthetic hand. Shaquem said this pushed him to prove that GM wrong.

Shaquem's combine performance got him praise on social media from football stars including Seattle Seahawks quarterback Russell Wilson and Houston Texans defensive end J. J. Watt.

A New Seattle Seahawks Star

After Shaquem's amazing combine performance, many were sure an NFL team would draft him. However, a draft spot—especially one by the Seattle Seahawks—wasn't a certainty. In April 2018, the Seattle Seahawks chose Shaquem as the 141st overall pick in the fifth round of the draft. He was reunited with Shaquill and their dream of playing together in the NFL came true.

UNSTOPPABLE!

During training camp, Shaquem said, "I got a lot to prove. I got to prove myself every single day, I'm not going to get comfortable where I'm at. I'm blessed and happy to be here, but the work is not done. Far from done."

Shaquem was watching the draft with his family when he got word that the Seahawks chose him. On April 28, 2018, Shaquem took the stage at AT&T Stadium in Arlington, Texas, as a player for the Seattle Seahawks with Shaquill.

Shaquem, who wears the number 49 jersey, continued to impress coaches and teammates at training camp practices. At one point, he intercepted a pass from quarterback Russell Wilson. He was a starting player in his first NFL game against the Broncos and played alongside Shaquill. Shaquem finished his rookie season with 18 tackles and had time on the field in every game.

A Future Inspiring Others

Becoming famous hasn't stopped Shaquem from giving back. He continues working to inspire children with disabilities to pursue their dreams. In February 2019, Shaquem visited Brooks **Rehabilitation** Center in Jacksonville, Florida, to meet patients with similar conditions and to show them that there's nothing they can't achieve.

Griffin hopes to encourage all others living with disabilities to let nothing hold them back from doing what they love and achieving their goals. Released in July 2019, Shaquem and Shaquill's book *Inseparable* tells about their journey to playing for the NFL and their family's unwavering support. In his open letter to NFL GMs, Shaquem thanked those who doubt him, because, "you're what keeps me motivated every day to work hard and play even harder."

UNSTOPPABLE!
Shaquem played 16 games at outside linebacker in the 2019 season. He recorded a sack on quarterback Aaron Rodgers in the divisional playoff game!

Griffin was named the winner of the Game Changer Award at the NFL Honors ceremony. This award is given to people in the football family who have positively contributed to football and their community.

TIMELINE

July 20, 1995
Shaquem and Shaquill are born around a minute apart.

1999
Griffin's left hand is amputated.

2016
Griffin receives American Athletic Conference Defensive Player of the Year honors.

2017
Griffin helps lead UCF to an undefeated season.

January 30, 2018
Shaquem receives an NFL Combine invite.

April 28, 2018
Griffin makes history as the first one-handed player to be drafted by an NFL team when the Seattle Seahawks pick him.

January 23, 2019
Shaquem accepts the NCAA Inspiration Award.

February 2019
Shaquem gives a speech and receives the Game Changer Award during the NFL Honors ceremony.

GLOSSARY

amputate: To cut off (part of a person's body).

congenital: Acquired during development in the womb and not from the parents' genes.

defensive: Of or relating to the way that players try to stop an opponent from scoring in a game or contest.

demote: To change the rank or position of someone to a lower or less important one.

intense: Existing to an extreme degree.

lobby: To try to get something you want by talking to the people who make decisions.

pact: A formal agreement between two people to help each other.

prosthetic: Of or relating to an artificial device that replaces a missing or injured part of the body.

rehabilitation: Relating to the act of bringing someone back to a normal, healthy condition after an illness or injury.

rookie: A first-year player in a professional sport.

scholarship: Money given to a student to help pay for further education.

ultrasound: A method of producing images of the inside of the body by using a machine that produces sound waves which are too high to be heard.

womb: Uterus, or the organ in women and female mammals in which the young develop before birth.

INDEX

WEBSITES

Due to the changing nature of Internet links, PowerKids Press has developed an online list of websites related to the subject of this book. This site is updated regularly. Please use this link to access the list: www.powerkidslinks.com/dcsu/griffin